Online Predators and Privacy

Eric Minton

PowerKiDS press

New York

hing Group, Inc.

)10

hing Group, Inc.

may be reproduced in any form without permission in writing
by a reviewer.

First Edition

Editor: Amelie von Zumbusch
Photo Research: Katie Stryker
Book Design: Colleen Bialecki
Book Layout: Andrew Povolny

Photo Credits: Cover, pp. 13, 25, 27 iStock/Thinkstock; p. 5 BunnyHollywood/The Agency Collection/
Getty Images; p. 6 Photodisc/Thinkstock; pp. 7, 19 Stockbyte/Thinkstock; p. 8 Kasia Baumann/Flickr
Open/Getty Images; p. 9 Dan Gair/Photolibrary/Getty Images; p. 10 Monkey Business/Thinkstock;
pp. 11, 28 Fuse/Thinkstock; pp. 12, 15, 29 Blend Images/Thinkstock; p. 16 Lane Oatey/Blue Jean
Images/Getty Images; p. 17 Maria Bobrova/E+/Getty Images; p. 20 Cultra/Atta=Fotografie/
The Images Bank/Getty Images; p. 21 Comstock Images/Getty Images; p. 23 Photodisc/Thinkstock;
p. 24 Blend Images/Ronnie Kaufman/The Agency Collection/Getty Images.

Library of Congress Cataloging-in-Publication Data

Minton, Eric.
 Online predators and privacy / by Eric Minton. — First edition.
    pages cm. — (Stay safe online)
Includes index.
 ISBN 978-1-4777-2940-3 (library binding) — ISBN 978-1-4777-3023-2 (pbk.) —
ISBN 978-1-4777-3094-2 (6-pack)
1. Internet—Safety measures. 2. Internet and children. 3. Privacy, Right of. 4. Computer
crimes. 5. Cyberbullying. 6. Online sexual
predators. I. Title.
 HQ784.I58M56 2014
 004.67'80835—dc23

                              2013033120

Manufactured in the United States of America

CPSIA Compliance Information: Batch # W14PK2: For Further Information contact Rosen Publishing, New York, New York at 1-800-237-9932

Contents

The Internet is more dangerous than you might think. Bullies can harass you online. Embarrassing messages, photos, or videos can hang around forever. You may even find yourself targeted by **scammers**, thieves, **hackers**, or online predators.

Online predators are people who lie to kids so that they can get close enough to do hurtful or inappropriate things to them. Few people are predators. You may never meet one. Because they're uncommon, though, it's easy to forget they're out there.

Your online privacy is how much you're able to control the things other people can see about you online. If you're not careful, strangers can use the Internet to learn where you live, what you're thinking, and more. That's why you need to protect your online privacy.

Be cautious with strangers online. If something about a person you're talking to online doesn't seem right, keep your distance.

Safe and Unsafe Places

Some places online are more private than others. On a **social media** site like Tumblr or Instagram, anyone can ask to join your network. Friends of your friends or even total strangers can be part of your network.

On online forums and blogs, you can see what other people are interested in by reading their posts. It's easy to start a conversation and make friends with someone who shares the same hobbies. You can also talk to people in real time by visiting a **chat room**.

Many social networks let you limit who can see your profile and posts. For example, you can set it so just friends, and not friends of friends, can see what you have written.

Be selective about accepting friend requests. It's not rude to turn down a friend request from a person you don't know. In fact, it's smart.

Online games, such as Space Heroes Universe or Club Penguin, let you chat with other players. Games for kids often limit the kinds of things that players can say. This is meant to make it harder for bullies and predators to take advantage.

Some online places protect your privacy better than others do. Learn whether a website or game is safe before spending time there.

Many social media sites, chat rooms, forums, and online games have **moderators**. Moderators are people whose job it is to prevent bullying and bad language. A moderator can delete inappropriate posts or ban troublemakers from a game or website. If you visit moderated sites, you're less likely to run into predators.

If another player in an online game that you play says something inappropriate, contact the moderator immediately.

Age limits are in place to keep kids safe. Social media sites aren't the only things that have them. Amusement park rides, movies, and many other things do, too.

Many social media sites let you make a profile only if you're at least 13 years old. These sites erase the accounts of underage users. Choose a social media site that allows younger users, such as Everloop or Yoursphere.

Did You Know?

More than half of all kids targeted by online predators were approached in chat rooms. Be extra careful about whom you talk to in chat rooms.

On the Internet, people have **anonymity**. This means that others don't know who they really are. You can't know for sure whether someone online is telling the truth about herself. For example, someone you think is a 13-year-old girl could be a 50-year-old man. A stranger can use tricks to make you think that he is someone other than himself. He can send you fake photos. He can send you texts or emails from a stolen phone or hacked email account.

Not using your real name in your email address or user name is one thing that you can do to protect your anonymity online.

When you meet people in person, it is easy to figure out certain things about them with your own two eyes. This is not the case for people you meet online.

Your own anonymity online can help protect you from dangerous people. It keeps them from finding out exactly who and where you are. Your anonymity is never complete, though. You may let slip clues. Someone may hack into your computer to steal your personal information.

Cookies and Spyware

Computer programs and smartphone **apps** can learn things about you in many ways. Often you won't even know that it is happening.

Many websites store information about you on your **web browser** in a file called a cookie. Browser cookies can store information like your name, passwords, or a list of things you've bought online. Websites use the information in browser cookies to show you advertisements for things that they think you might want to buy.

Cookies invade your privacy but are less of a risk than malware is. Most companies that use cookies want to use the information they get to make money, not to steal it.

If you do online searches for information about horses, you might get ads for riding equipment. This happens because of the cookies in your browser.

Malware is any kind of computer program that collects information from your computer to use in damaging ways. The owner of a malware program can use it to steal your passwords and other personal information. Malware includes **viruses** that can slow down your computer or erase files.

Never post anything on the Internet that a stranger could use to find you. This includes your real name, age, home address, phone number, and school. Don't say when or where you'll be in a public place.

Always turn off location sharing in smartphone apps. Turn on your phone's global positioning system, or GPS, only when you need it. Turn the GPS off right away when you're done with it.

Never take photos while your phone's GPS is on. Your phone's camera hides location information in every photo. Online predators can use this to see where a photo was taken. Don't post photos or videos of yourself online. Don't talk to strangers by video. Keep your webcam turned off.

Don't share your date of birth online. Predators can use it to figure out how old you are. Scammers can use it to try to get into your accounts.

It is easy to share information about yourself online accidentally. Read your messages and posts carefully to make sure you don't reveal anything important. Social media sites have **privacy settings** that control who can see your posts. Use them to block strangers.

It is fun to take photos of yourself and friends. Just be careful about where those photos end up.

It is okay to mention that you do martial arts online. However, you should not mention the name of the martial-arts school that you attend.

Don't post anything that a stranger could use to find you. Photos and videos of your neighborhood may include clues, such as street signs, business names, and local landmarks. Posts about local events, such as concerts or football games, also provide clues.

Other people may take photos or videos of you and post them online. If you see someone taking pictures of you, ask her not to post them. If you see pictures of yourself online, ask the owner to take them down.

Online predators act extra nice to get you to trust them. They will praise you and act interested in everything that you say. Some will even send you gifts.

A predator will agree with you on almost everything. He will pretend to like the same things you do, such as the same movies, music, or sports. The predator may try to convince you that your family can't understand you or your problems and that only he can understand you.

To get closer to you, a predator will want to talk to you by phone or video. Eventually he will likely want to meet you in person. Never meet a stranger without a parent or other trusted adult around.

A predator may try to get his victim to distance herself from friends and family members. The predator hopes that he will be the only person the victim has to turn to.

Did You Know?

Predators aren't real friends. They aren't actually interested in you as a person. They just want to win your trust in order to get close to you.

19

If a stranger contacts you online, don't respond. Tell a trustworthy adult immediately. Don't read the stranger's messages or open any files. Save those messages and files as **evidence**.

On a social media site, you can block messages from a predator. You can also report her to the site's owners. Some phone service providers let you block someone from calling you or sending you text messages. To find out how, call the provider or look for instructions online.

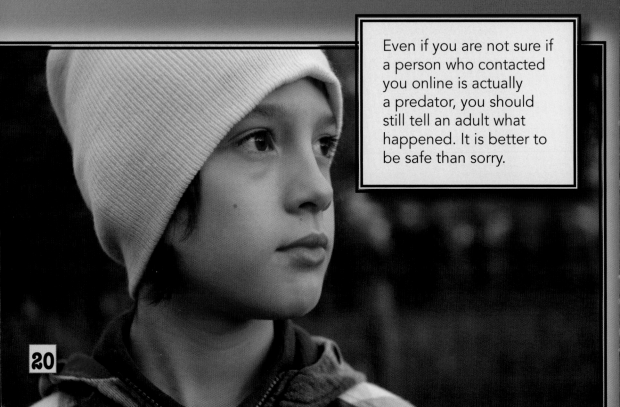

Even if you are not sure if a person who contacted you online is actually a predator, you should still tell an adult what happened. It is better to be safe than sorry.

Never open any attachments from a stranger, especially if you think that person may be an online predator. Predators often send kids upsetting photos and videos.

Predators try to control kids in several ways. A predator may threaten to tell a kid's parents about their relationship. Predators also say that kids will get in trouble if they tell anyone about the predator. In truth, predators who say these things are just trying to protect themselves.

Did You Know?

Predators may ask you to take pictures of yourself. If that happens, tell a trusted adult right away and do not send any pictures.

If a stranger does anything to you that makes you uncomfortable or ashamed, remember that it wasn't your fault. You're still a good person. The predator is the bad guy, not you.

Talk to an adult you trust about what happened. Sorting out your feelings about a bad experience like this can be confusing. It will help you to talk about what happened and how it made you feel. Therapists and counselors are people trained to help you deal with big problems. It can help to spend time talking to one on a regular basis while you sort things out.

Don't let an experience with a predator spoil the Internet for you. You can still have fun online, as long as you're careful.

If an experience with an online predator is still upsetting you a while after it happened, talk to a parent about finding a therapist or counselor to whom you can talk.

Did You Know?

If a grown-up does or says something to you that you're ashamed of, don't pretend that nothing happened. Get help from your parents or some other adult you trust.

23

Catching Predators

If you think you're dealing with an online predator, remember that predators are criminals. They can be dangerous. You and your parents should never confront a predator yourselves. This is a job for the police.

It's important to keep all of a predator's messages, photos, and videos as evidence. The police will use this evidence to identify the predator. It may also be used to convict the predator in court and send him to jail.

If a predator sent you messages on your phone, your parents may need to take the phone to the police.

Save copies of every email, text, photo, and video a predator sends you. If you use an instant messaging program, set it to keep a **log** of all your conversations. Take a **screenshot** of any message you can't save or log. This includes messages in chat rooms and online video games.

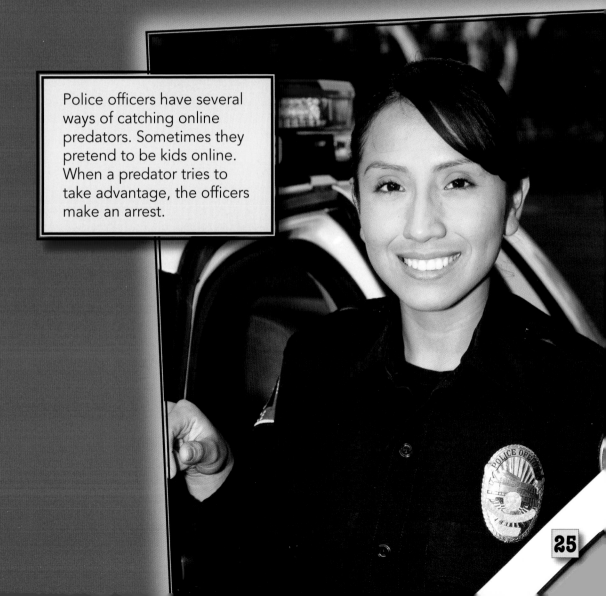

Police officers have several ways of catching online predators. Sometimes they pretend to be kids online. When a predator tries to take advantage, the officers make an arrest.

The Internet is also home to scammers and thieves. They will try to trick you into giving information they can use to get money. Never give out your family's credit card numbers or bank account numbers online. Thieves use those numbers to buy things with your family's money.

Never give out your social security number. A criminal can use that number to pretend to be you. This is called **identity theft**. If someone commits crimes or owes money under your name, you may be held responsible. When you're older, you may find it harder to get a driver's license or credit card.

Scammers always have good stories about why they want your personal information. Don't give out that information, no matter what anyone says.

If a credit card company contacts you about a credit card, tell an adult immediately. A scammer may have set up an account with your name on it.

Did You Know?

Never give out any kind of personal information, such as passwords or credit card numbers, in response to an email.

27

Cyberbullies are people who bully online. The more they learn about you, the easier it is for them to bully you. Talking online about embarrassing events or feelings can make you a target for bullies. Getting into arguments online can, too.

Don't let friends draw you into cyberbullying. Leaving mean comments on a post is cyberbullying. Convincing others to unfriend someone on a social network is, too.

When someone bullies you online, start by ignoring her. Some bullies just want attention and will go away if they don't get it. If a bully keeps bothering you, tell your parents or another trusted adult. Don't read bullying messages and posts, but keep copies of them as evidence.

Whether you're dealing with cyberbullies, Internet predators, or identity thieves, staying private helps you stay safe online. The less that people can learn about you, the better.

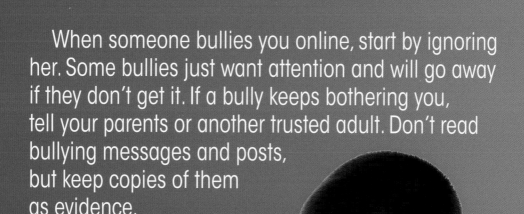

Though some people online are untrustworthy, plenty of others can be trusted. Don't let the bad people online scare you off the Internet entirely.

1. Make sure your screen name doesn't say anything about you, such as your age, nickname, or whether you're a boy or girl.

2. Trust your feelings about what kinds of words or pictures are okay and what kinds aren't. Avoid anything that makes you uncomfortable.

3. Don't answer questions that make you uncomfortable or could be used to find where you live. If someone insists, stop talking to him or her.

4. If a stranger asks you not to tell anyone about your relationship with him, this is a big warning sign! Tell a trusted adult immediately.

5. Any conversation you have online can be recorded. This includes instant messages, voice chats, and conversations in chat rooms and with webcams.

6. If a stranger gives you her phone number, don't call. A predator can learn your phone number from your call.

7. Don't assume that someone's safe to talk to because they look or sound normal. Predators and scammers can be as friendly and charming as anyone.

Glossary

anonymity (a-nuh-NIH-muh-tee) The state of not being known.

apps (APS) Computer programs made for mobile devices, such as smartphones and tablets.

chat room (CHAT ROOM) An online place where people can type messages to each other.

evidence (EH-vuh-dunts) Facts that prove something.

hackers (HA-kerz) People who break into email accounts or other computer systems.

identity theft (eye-DEN-tuh-tee THEFT) Pretending to be someone else in order to open accounts in that person's name.

log (LOG) A record of day-to-day activities.

moderators (MO-deh-ray-turz) People who make sure others are getting along on a website.

privacy settings (PRY-vuh-see SEH-tingz) The way to choose who can see different parts of your profile or posts on social media sites.

scammers (SKAM-erz) People who try to trick people into doing things.

screenshot (SKREEN-shot) A picture of what is on a computer screen.

social media (SOH-shul MEE-dee-uh) Having to do with online communities through which people share information, messages, photos, videos, and thoughts.

viruses (VY-rus-ez) Programs that harm a computer.

web browser (WEB BROW-zur) A computer program used to view websites.

Index

Websites

Due to the changing nature of Internet links, PowerKids Press has developed an online list of websites related to the subject of this book. This site is updated regularly. Please use this link to access the list: www.powerkidslinks.com/sso/predat/